BIG
BIG BUGS

by Catherine Ipcizade

Consulting Editor: Gail Saunders-Smith, PhD

Consultant: Gary Dunn, MS, Executive Director
Young Entomologists' Society Inc.
Lansing, Michigan

Capstone press

Mankato, Minnesota

Pebble Plus is published by Capstone Press,
151 Good Counsel Drive, P.O. Box 669, Mankato, Minnesota 56002.
www.capstonepress.com

Books published by Capstone Press are manufactured with paper
containing at least 10 percent post-consumer waste.

Library of Congress Cataloging-in-Publication Data
Ipcizade, Catherine.
    Big bugs / by Catherine Ipcizade.
    p. cm. — (Pebble plus. big)
    Includes bibliographical references and index.
    ISBN 978-1-4296-3317-8 (library binding)
1. Insects — Size — Juvenile literature. I. Title. II. Series.
QL467.2I68 2010
595.7 — dc22   2009001614

Summary: Simple text and photographs describe big bugs.

Editorial Credits
Erika L. Shores, editor; Ted Williams, designer; Jo Miller, media researcher

Photo Credits
Alamy/Rick & Nora Bowers, 9
AP Images/Chiang Liang-yi, 17
Peter Arnold/BIOS Bios/Auteurs Cavignaux Bruno, 21; Biosphoto/Cordier Sylvain, 13; Biosphoto/Montford Thierry, 5;
    Georges Lopez, cover; James Gerholdt, 19; S. J. Krasemann, 11
Photo Researchers, Inc/John Mitchell, 7
Shutterstock/Cathy Keifer, 15; javarman, cover (background); Markov, cover (bug background); Steve Smith
    Photography, 1

Note to Parents and Teachers

The Big set supports national science standards related to life science. This book describes and
illustrates big bugs. The images support early readers in understanding the text. The repetition
of words and phrases helps early readers learn new words. This book also introduces early
readers to subject-specific vocabulary words, which are defined in the Glossary section. Early
readers may need assistance to read some words and to use the Table of Contents, Glossary,
Read More, Internet Sites, and Index sections of the book.

Table of Contents

Big

Big legs! Big fangs!
All kinds of big parts
help bugs survive.

A tarantula's leg span
can be up to 12 inches
(30 centimeters).

Giant water bugs use
big front legs to trap frogs.

Size:

up to 2.5 inches
(6 centimeters) long

Tarantula hawks are wasps
with big wings.
They sting tarantulas
then lay eggs on them.

Size:

4-inch (10-centimeter) wingspan

9

Bigger

Big yellow and black wings
keep imperial moths safe.
Their wings blend in with trees.
Predators can't spot the moths.

Size:

5-inch (13-centimeter) wingspan

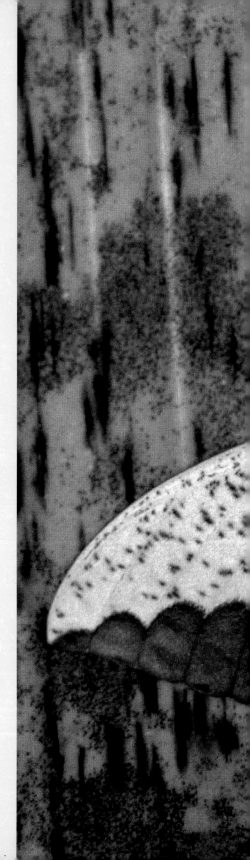

11

Peanut-head bugs have

spots on their wings.

The spots look like big eyes.

They scare away predators.

Size:

6-inch (15-centimeter) wingspan

13

Biggest

Praying mantises use
big, spiky front legs
to catch crickets.

Size:
up to 6 inches
(15 centimeters) long

Male Atlas beetles jab
each other with big horns.
They fight for a mate.

Size:

up to 5 inches
(13 centimeters) long

Scorpions hunt at night.
Their long tails jab prey
with a big sting.

Size:
up to 6 inches
(15 centimeters) long

Goliath bird-eating spiders
hide during the day.
They hunt at night.
Their big fangs sink into prey.

Size:
up to 12-inch
(30-centimeter) leg span

Glossary

blend — to fit in with surroundings

fang — a long, hollow tooth; a poison called venom flows through fangs.

jab — to poke very quickly

mate — the male or female partner of a pair of animals

predator — an animal that hunts other animals for food

prey — an animal hunted by another animal for food

sting — to hurt with a poisoned tip

survive — to stay alive

Read More

McNab, Chris. *Giant Spiders & Insects.* Nature's Monsters: Insects & Spiders. Milwaukee: Gareth Stevens, 2007.

Simon, Seymour. *Big Bugs.* SeeMore Readers. San Francisco: SeaStar Books, 2005.

Internet Sites

FactHound offers a safe, fun way to find Internet sites related to this book. All of the sites on FactHound have been researched by our staff.

Here's all you do:

Visit *www.facthound.com*

FactHound will fetch the best sites for you!

Index

Word Count: 128
Grade: 1
Early-Intervention Level: 16

24